Withdrawn

by Adam Markovics

Consultant: Marjorie Faulstich Orellana, PhD
Professor of Urban Schooling
University of California, Los Angeles

New York, New York

Credits

Cover, © New Africa/Shutterstock and © Mariusz Switulski; TOC, © Kamenetskiy Konstantin/Shutterstock; 4, © Nicolas Alexander Otto/Alamy; 5L, © seier + seier/CC BY 4.0; 5R, © Westend61 GmbH/Alamy; 7, © EyesTravelling/Shutterstock; 8, © Dhoxax/iStock; 9T, © Dr. Christa Lüdecke/imageBROKER/Alamy; 9B, © Patrik Paulinyi/Shutterstock; 10, © jonathanfilskov-photography/iStock; 11T, © Rudmer Zwerver/Shutterstock; 11B, © Piotr Krzeslak/Shutterstock; 12, © Valentina Photo/Shutterstock; 13T, © emka74/Shutterstock; 13B, © Tory Kallman/Shutterstock; 14T, © CM Dixon Heritage Images/Newscom; 14B, © E. Klein Internet Archive Book Images; 15, © maradon 333/Shutterstock; 16L, © scanrail/iStock; 16–17, © Leonid Andronov/iStock; 18, © Jaroslav Moravcik/Shutterstock; 19, © Jean Schweitzer energy pictures/Alamy; 20, © Aleksandr Volkov/Dreamstime; 21, © miljko/iStock; 22, © skynesher/iStock; 23, © skynesher/iStock; 24L, © Michael715/Shutterstock; 24–25, © Magdanatka/Shutterstock; 26, © db2stock/iStock; 27, © CARTA image/Alamy; 28, © Anastasia Pelikh/Shutterstock; 29, © studiolaska/Shutterstock; 30T, © Oleksiy Mark/Shutterstock and © Yaroslaff/Shutterstock; 30B, © Aaron Amat/Shutterstock; 31 (T to B), © Hamish Gray/Shutterstock, © Dusan Petkovic/Shutterstock, © Ivychuang1101/Shutterstock, © saiko3p/Shutterstock, © Kichigin/Shutterstock, and © Lorado/Shutterstock; 32, © neftali/Shutterstock.

Publisher: Kenn Goin
Senior Editor: Joyce Tavolacci
Creative Director: Spencer Brinker
Design: Debrah Kaiser
Photo Researcher: Thomas Persano

Library of Congress Cataloging-in-Publication Data

Names: Markovics, Adam, author.
Title: Denmark / by Adam Markovics.
Description: New York, New York: Bearport Publishing Company, Inc., [2020] |
  Series: Countries we come from | Includes bibliographical references and
  index.
Identifiers: LCCN 2019010061 (print) | LCCN 2019011833 (ebook) | ISBN
  9781642805765 (ebook) | ISBN 9781642805222 (library)
Subjects: LCSH: Denmark—Juvenile literature.
Classification: LCC DL109 (ebook) | LCC DL109 .M37 2019 (print) | DDC
  948.9—dc23
LC record available at https://lccn.loc.gov/2019010061

For more information, write to Bearport Publishing Company, Inc., 45 West 21st Street, Suite 3B, New York, New York 10010. Printed in the United States of America.

10 9 8 7 6 5 4 3 2 1

Contents

BREATHTAKING

Bold

Friendly

Denmark is a small country in Europe.

It sits on a **peninsula** and includes over 400 islands!

Jutland Peninsula

Denmark

EUROPE

Arctic Ocean

NORTH AMERICA

EUROPE

ASIA

Atlantic Ocean

Pacific Ocean

AFRICA

Pacific Ocean

SOUTH AMERICA

Indian Ocean

N

W   E

S

AUSTRALIA

Southern Ocean

ANTARCTICA

Nearly six million people call Denmark home. The people of Denmark are often called Danes.

Denmark is mostly flat, with green rolling hills.

Long ago, **glaciers** shaped Denmark's land.

They created long, deep waterways called fjords (FEE-ords).

glacier

moraine

fjord

Glaciers left behind piles of rocks and earth known as moraines (muh-REYNZ).

Denmark's largest land animal is the red deer.

The country's strangest animal may be the slow worm.

It looks like a snake, but it's actually a legless lizard!

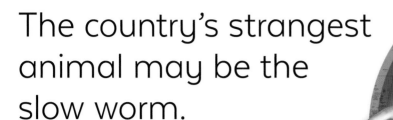

Eurasian jay

Three hundred kinds of birds live in Denmark.

Denmark is famous for its ocean life.

Cod, herring, and shellfish thrive in the ocean waters.

cod

Seals dive in the sea and then rest on the shore.

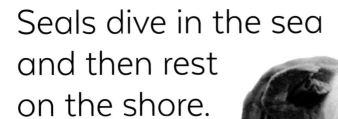

Killer whales, or orcas, swim off Denmark's coast.

13

For 100,000 years, people have lived in Denmark.

The Vikings lived there over 1,000 years ago.

The Vikings were **warriors** who sailed on ships.

a model of a Viking ship

The Vikings held power for about 300 years.

15

The **capital** of Denmark is Copenhagen.

The city is located on a big island.

It used to be a Viking fishing village.

Copenhagen is Denmark's largest city. Nearly one million people live there.

To get around Denmark, people ride bikes.

Some Danish cities have more bikes than people!

Many Danes bike to work or school.

There are thousands of miles of bike paths in Denmark.

19

Danish people love the cold!
Some Danes swim in winter.
They jump right into icy water.

The winter swimmers
are nicknamed "Vikings."

Then, people warm up in hot **saunas**.

The main language in Denmark is Danish.

This is how you say *good day* in Danish:

Goddag (GOH-day)

This is how you say *thank you*:

Tak (TACK)

Many Danes also speak English.

Danish food is delicious!

People enjoy open sandwiches called smørrebrød (SMUHR-bruth).

The sandwiches are often eaten on dark rye bread.

Denmark is known for its buttery cookies and pastries.

24

Legos come from Denmark.
A Danish **carpenter** invented
them around 1930.

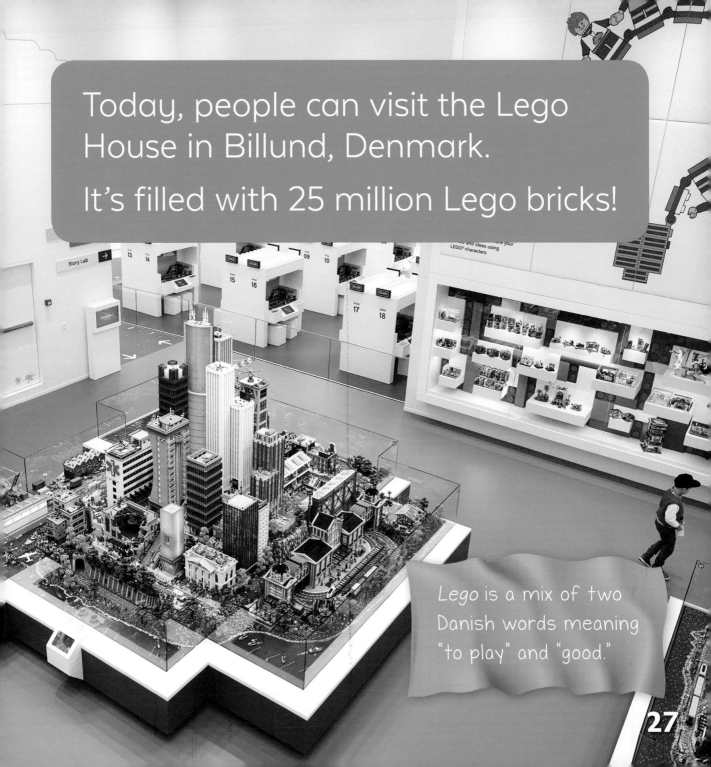

Today, people can visit the Lego House in Billund, Denmark.

It's filled with 25 million Lego bricks!

Lego is a mix of two Danish words meaning "to play" and "good."

Let's have fun!
Danes love Tivoli Gardens.

Denmark has been named one of the happiest places on earth.

It's one of the oldest amusement parks in the world!

It has four roller coasters and dozens of other rides.

Tivoli Gardens opened in 1843.

Fast Facts

Capital city:
Copenhagen

Population of Denmark:
Nearly six million

Main language: Danish

Money: Danish kroner

Major religion: Christian

Neighboring country: Germany

Cool Fact: Danes love eating salty licorice with a glass of cold milk!

Glossary

capital (KAP-uh-tuhl) the city where a country's government is based

carpenter (KAHR-puhn-tur) someone who works with wood

glaciers (GLAY-shurz) huge, slow-moving sheets of ice

peninsula (puh-NIN-suh-la) a piece of land that sticks out from a larger land mass and is almost completely surrounded by water

saunas (SAW-nuhs) baths that use dry or steam heat

warriors (WOR-ee-urz) soldiers who are experienced in fighting battles

Index

Read More

Gifford, Clive. *Denmark (Unpacked).* London: Wayland (2017).

Zobel, Derek. *Denmark (Exploring Countries).* Minneapolis, MN: Bellwether (2011).

Learn More Online

To learn more about Denmark, visit
www.bearportpublishing.com/CountriesWeComeFrom

About the Author

Adam Markovics lives in Ossining, New York. He loves Danish design and hopes to visit Denmark with his wife, Joyce, before the start of the twenty-second century.